stations of the cross

Volume 1: I am the WAY

By Brother Peter Huynh, LC

In collaboration with

14 seminarians

and

14 KIDS

volume 1:

i am the WAY

BY BROTHER PETER HUYNH, LC

When you browse through these pages, what do you make of these drawings? At first glance, these seem like a mess of clashing colors, thick rough lines, shocking shapes, disturbing disproportions and debris of crayons scattered randomly over the page.

Some of these make you either giggle, skew your eyebrows, or squeal: "Awww! That's adorable!" That's the way adults see things. Of course at-first-glance.

However, children see things a bit differently. Children see the same things adults do, but how they express what they perceive is totally unique. Their minds are like clean sponges. They soak up the colors, images, concepts, and feelings which they see. Their senses take in every new impulse, and their curiosity grows. Children's emotions are honest and sincere. They have no need to cover them with complicated prejudice or jealousy. When a little girl sees Christ carrying the cross, she simply perceives "a good man is getting hurt for something he didn't do. And that's not fair!"

A child may not know how to get a man on the moon, program in JavaScript, open a bank account, or make dinner without using the microwave. However, that same child can express in an illustration his deep feelings of what Christ endured on his way to Calvary. What you see is their unadulterated view of what Christ did for them. The boyish, melancholic grey and brown speak of a fight between love and hate. A girl chooses bright blue, cheerful canary, and floral fuchsia which convey the kindness and love with which Jesus embraces the cross.

In this book, young men studying for the priesthood share their reflections on the Stations of the Cross. The seminarians wrap their reflections with such a simple and bite-size language that it is easy for the young readers to chew on. The winning artworks of the "2012 Stations of the Cross Drawing Contest" accompany these reflections. These young artists and young seminarians form quite a team! The best of creed, color, catechism, crayons, and creativity are all bound in this book to help young readers accompany Christ during Lent.

Adults have as much to learn from children as they, from us. The whole message of carrying the cross is one of total self-giving. From the cross, Christ beckons us to love as he loves. And this is my prayer: that all of us correspond generously to his Love this Lent by picking up our crosses and following him.

"Unless you are converted and become like children, you will not enter the kingdom of heaven." Matthew 18:3

how to pray the stations of the cross

1. Pray the Stations of the Cross in a place where they are displayed, for instance in a Church, outside, or even in your classroom.

2. One person carries a cross and stops at each Station for a moment of reflection. An appropriate reading, like the ones presented in this booklet, may serve as a helpful guide.

3. One of the readers announces each Station, saying for example, "The Second Station: Jesus carries his cross."

3. Another reader says, "We adore you Christ, and we praise you."

4. To this invocation the whole assembly answers, "Because by your holy cross, you have redeemed the world."

5. Different readers can read the three parts offered for each Station: the quote from the Bible, the reflection and the prayer written by a seminarian.

Pilate had Jesus brought out, and seated himself on the chair of judgment at a place called the Pavement, in Hebrew *Gabbatha*.

-from the Gospel of St. John 19:13

JESUS IS CONDEMNED TO DEATH

reflection by:
Brother Csaba Szász, LC

artwork by:
Olivia
Third-place Winner
3rd grade
St. John the Baptist Catholic School
Longmont, CO, USA

1

first station

reflection:

The people are gathered together. Something important is happening before Pilate's palace. I draw near to the crowd to see what I can learn: On the stage, Pilate washes his hands with dignity, for a man with such authority is not allowed to make mistakes: "I'm innocent of this man's blood." (Mt 27,24) There were two men standing next to Pilate: one is Jesus, recently handed over to be crucified. "What have you done, my Lord? For which of your good deeds do they wish to crucify you?" While I ask this question, Scripture is being fulfilled: "The Lord laid upon him the guilt of us all. Though he was harshly treated, he submitted and opened not his mouth; Like a lamb led to the slaughter or a sheep before the shearers, he was silent and opened not his mouth." (Is 53, 66-67)

my prayer to Jesus:

Jesus, my Lord, my God, my All, how can I love thee as I ought? Teach me to look at your suffering face, when tempted to criticize others. Meek lamb of God, I beg of you, make my heart more like yours: humble, benign and loving.

And when they had mocked him, they stripped him of the cloak, dressed him in his own clothes, and led him off to crucify him.

-from the Gospel of St. Matthew
27:31

reflection by:
Brother Jeremy Lambert, LC

artwork by:
Andrew
First-Place Winner
3rd grade
Northwood Catholic School
Spring, TX, USA

2

second station

reflection:

A Roman soldier walked through the forest with an axe. He was looking for the straightest tree around. Right and left he saw twisted trunks and small saplings. All at once he came upon an old, noble and straight oak that reached to the sky. This was the one he had been searching for. Little did he know that this tree would soon be used to make the cross that Jesus would carry to his crucifixion and death. When Jesus carried the heavy cross on his shoulder it represented our sins. Every step under the weight of the cross was difficult, but he showed how much he loved each one of us.

my prayer to Jesus:

Jesus, when I see a cross in church, on the wall at home, or on a chain around someone's neck, I don't want to be indifferent. I wish to remember that the cross is a sign of your love for me. Help me to be more aware of what you suffered in my place, so that I wouldn't have to. Amen.

After withdrawing about a stone's throw from them and kneeling, he prayed, saying, "Father, if you are willing, take this cup away from me; still, not my will but yours be done."

-from the Gospel of St. Luke 22:41-42

reflection by:
Brother John Bender, LC

artwork by:
Katherine
Third-Place Winner
4th grade
Pinecrest Academy
Cumming, GA, USA

reflection:

Jesus was very tired. He hadn't slept all night. And yet he was forced to carry the heavy, wooden cross for a long time. It was hard to carry; awkward. And he fell, the cross landing on top of him, banging his head into the ground. It hurt. But no one was there to help him up. No one lifted the cross off his back, no one helped him stand back up, no one asked if he was all right. Instead they laughed at him, they pointed their fingers at him, they spat at him. "Jesus, Why? Why are you carrying the cross?" He didn't complain, he didn't talk back, he didn't get mad. He got back on his feet, picked up the cross, and kept going. Why? Because he loves me.

my prayer to Jesus:

Lord Jesus, how many times do people around me fall down— at school, during a game, at home—and I laugh at them, or point my finger at them, or I walk by without helping them up. Help me Lord to be more like you, who never ignored anyone who was in need. Teach me to love like you; teach me to help others. I love you Jesus. Thank you for loving me.

And his mother kept all these things in her heart

-from the Gospel
of St. Luke 2:51

4

fourth station

reflection by:
Brother Nicholas Fisher, LC

artwork by:
William

Second-Place Winner
5th grade
St. Thomas the Apostle
Miami, FL, USA

reflection:

Jesus carries his cross toward Calvary. All his muscles are tight and sore as though he were running in a race. He is tired, and in spite of his effort, he can barely move forward—the cross is so heavy. The sides of the road are crowded with people shouting, but very few of them are Jesus' fans. Most of them are booing him and laughing at his weakness. He is alone. Then he sees his mother in the crowd. Mary is there, watching and praying. She does not shout like the rest of the crowd. But Jesus can sense his mother's love and encouragement. Mary is there and he is not alone. And with this consolation, Jesus continues slowly on the road towards Calvary.

my prayer to Mary:

Mary, mother of Jesus and my mother, walk with me each day of my life and be near me in my moments of pain and fear. Watch over me and protect me, mother, from all harm, and lead me on the path to heaven. Amen.

As they were going out, they met a
Cyrenian named Simon; this man they
pressed into service to carry his cross.

-from the Gospel of St. Matthew 27:32

reflection by:
Brother Adrian Canal, LC

artwork by:
Joseph
TIED: First-Place Winner
3rd grade
Meadowlark Elementary
Kearney, NE, USA

5
fifth station

reflection:

At this point of the morning Jesus is totally exhausted. He had probably fallen more than once and he wasn't able to get up any more. Why? He hadn't slept the night before; he had eaten no breakfast; he had been scourged and had been forced to walk a long way to see Herod; he had lost a lot of blood. The Roman soldiers saw themselves in trouble. A sentence was given and they had to fulfill it. They had two options: either carry Jesus themselves or find someone strong enough to do it. They obviously preferred the second. Jesus was bloody, sweaty and dusty. It was repulsive to come near him. Right then a man was passing by. Simon was his name. He came from North Africa. He was big and strong, like a huge athlete. One of the soldiers pointed at him, drew his sword and yelled: "You there. Help his majesty: the King of the Jews, to carry his cross." Who would want to help a prisoner fulfill such a dirty punishment? Yet from behind a woman named Veronica came and whispered in his ear: "Simon, give him a hand. He is innocent. This man Jesus worked many miracles. They are jealous." Then he saw a group of Pharisees coming on their donkeys, a wicked look in their eyes. "Okay, woman. I'll help this Jesus carry the cross." "But, hey," he shouted out loud. "I am innocent. I did no evil to anyone. Hey all of you, I am not paying any penalty. I'll do this out of kindness. ... Let's go. Get up. I'll help you. Come on." As he took the cross and Jesus with it, Simon began to feel joyful. Then he looked into Jesus' eyes and his heart knew that this man was no criminal. At the end it was he who was motivating Jesus to arrive at the top of Calvary. That is the way it is when we do things for Christ. When we help a fellow who is in need, when we speak to the kid nobody likes, when we patiently help our little sister do her homework. Jesus is also expecting you to give him a hand by helping those around you. Will you say no?

Blessed are the merciful for they will be shown mercy. Blessed are the clean of heart for they will see God.

-from the Gospel of St. Matthew 5:7,8

VERONICA WIPES THE FACE OF JESUS

reflection by:
Brother Brian Coe, LC

artwork by:
Addison
Third-Place Winner
5th grade
John Paul Preparatory School
Ballwin, MO, USA

6

sixth station

reflection:

Jesus is trying to get up after collapsing under the weight of the cross. The sand and dust from the dirt road have mixed with the blood from the crown of thorns that oozes all over his face. Jesus wipes his eyes, but the gunk on his hands only makes it worse. Seeing this, a girl named Veronica decides that enough is enough. Defying the big, strong soldiers, she bolts towards Jesus. Everyone freezes and watches as she lovingly cleans off Jesus' face, getting the grime out of his mouth and eyes. Jesus' gaze meets hers, but his mouth is too dry to say anything. Veronica bursts into tears as he tries to mouth a message. She gives him a big hug and, sobbing, buries her face into his chest until the centurion approaches and shoves her aside. Jesus shoulders the cross again and heads off down the road. She is so sad; then she looks down and realizes that he had left her a miraculous "Thank You" note: a picture of his face on the cloth she cleaned him with.

But he was pierced for our transgressions, he was crushed for our iniquities; the punishment that brought us peace was upon him, and by his wounds we are healed.

-Isaiah 53:5

JESUS FALLS THE SECOND TIME

reflection by:
Brother Nicholas Sheehy, LC

artwork by:
Samantha
First-place Winner
3rd grade
St. Thomas More School
Decatur, GA, USA

7

seventh station

reflection:

Do you ever feel like everybody is on your case? As Jesus falls the second time on the Way of the Cross, he is for us an example of faith and hope. He had been scourged and lost blood. The crowd is shouting at him. The soldiers are pushing him. He feels light-headed and falls to the ground. The heavy cross falls on top of him, adding to the pain. Why does Jesus fall on the Way of the Cross? He falls so he can get back up and show us how to respond to failure in our own lives. Bad things happen in life but we can keep living if we love Christ and keep our eyes fixed on the cross.

my prayer to Jesus:

Lord Jesus Christ, you see that I am weak. I often do not feel like being the hero. But I know that you just want me to do my best. When those around me are complaining or giving in to temptation, help me to be strong and to get up and to follow you. Help me to love you more each day.

To the poor lend an ear and courteously return the greeting.

-Ecclesiasticus 4:8

reflection by:
Brother David Barton, LC

artwork by:
Katie
Second-Place Winner
4th grade
St. John the Baptist Catholic School
Longmont, CO, USA

reflection:

As Jesus carries his cross on the path that leads to the hill where they will crucify him, he turns the corner and finds a group of women who are crying because of the pain that they see Jesus suffering. These women do not want Jesus to die—they love him so much that it breaks their hearts to see him suffering and bleeding.

Most of us have had the experience of falling off our bikes and scraping up our knees or elbows. After we get cleaned up, we take pride in showing off our cuts and bruises to our friends because they make us look like a hero, and we want people to think that we are great because we survived the fall. Even though Jesus *is* the hero, he did not want these women to feel sorry for him—he loves us so much that when he hurts the most, he still wants to love more without looking for anything in return. Jesus loves us so much that he does not even worry about how much he hurts—all he can think of is how to love us more.

my prayer to Jesus:

Jesus, sometimes when things are hard I want others to feel sorry for me or to try to cheer me up. Help me to take those moments that are difficult and give them to you as an act of love. Don't let me be selfish by thinking of how hard things are at times, but let me always count my blessings and thank you for all the love that you have shown to me as my father and friend.

At this I weep, my eyes run with tears:
Far from me are all who could console
me, any who might revive me; My sons
were reduced to silence when the
enemy prevailed.

-Lamentations 1:16

JESUS FALLS THE THIRD TIME

9

reflection by:
Brother José Eduardo Sánchez, LC

artwork by:
Nick
Second-Place Winner
3rd grade
Blessed Sacrament School
Wichita, KS, USA

ninth station

reflection:

The number three in the Bible could mean *many times*. When we consider Jesus falling for the third time, we are saying, Jesus fell many times. Why? Jesus wanted to teach us what our attitude should be towards our falls in our struggle to reach heaven: We should get up and keep fighting. By experience we know that we do not always behave well, falling many times into temptation. To fall down is normal, it's part of our human condition. But the important thing is not the fall, but not to remain on the ground, to stand up and recognize our mistakes, to ask God to forgive us and to keep going in our way to heaven, loving Jesus as our best friend.

my prayer to Jesus:

Lord Jesus, you knew that in our life we fall many times. That's why you also wanted to experience the pain and humiliation of falling many times. We ask you to help us persevere in the fight to reach heaven, not looking at our weaknesses and falls, but at the reward you have promised us.

Amen, I say to you, today you will be with me in Paradise.

-from the Gospel of St. Luke 23:43

JESUS IS STRIPPED OF HIS GARMENTS

reflection by:
Brother Peter Mullan, LC

artwork by:
Giselle
First-Place Winner
4th grade
Pinecrest Academy
Cumming, GA, USA

tenth station

reflection:

After a long, tiring walk up the hill of Calvary, carrying his cross the entire way, Jesus finally makes it to the top. He can hardly stand any more. Before nailing him to the cross, the soldiers find one more way to make fun of him: they strip off his outer clothing, leaving him almost naked in front of the entire crowd. Jesus' wounds begin to bleed again. If it hurts us when we rip a band-aid off of a small cut, imagine how much it hurt Christ, whose entire body had become one big sore! When others laugh at us and make fun of us, we feel more pain than if they were to punch us. Jesus, however, accepts all the mean laughter, knowing that his Father sees him and loves him. And he does it for us, so that we too can put up with others making fun of us, when we know we are doing what God wants.

my prayer to Jesus:

Dear Jesus, how hard it is for you to carry out your Father's plan! Couldn't there be any easier way? Many times I try to find easier ways than what I know I should do, especially when I know others will laugh at me. Help me to stick it out, knowing that I will be happiest doing what God wants of me. He is my good Father; teach me to trust him! Amen.

There they crucified him, and with him two others, one on either side, with Jesus in the middle.

-from the Gospel of St. John 19:18

JESUS IS NAILED TO THE CROSS

reflection by:
Brother Mark Thelen, LC

artwork by:
Paulina
First-Place Winner
5th grade
St. Thomas the Apostle
Miami, FL, USA

11

eleventh station

reflection:

It's a mystery—Jesus, God, is nailed to a cross! What does the cross mean for him and why does he hang there? Now Jesus and his cross are inseparable. Imagine Jesus picking up and embracing his cross—his instrument of torture and death, a sign of his condemnation. Yet his love for the cross becomes complete when he is nailed to it. In reality, it is not iron through his hands and feet that hold him fast but rather love for the Father and for us that will never permit him to come down. So many times I want to cast off my cross. It seems that I am forced to bear it, but I only need to love. Then, and only then, does it become the most meaningful thing in my life, uniting me to Christ and his redeeming love.

my prayer to Jesus:

Jesus, you hung on the cross out of love for me. My sins should have nailed me to the cross. Yet in love, you took my place. Your pure, unconditional, and divine love held you fast to the wood of the saving cross. Give me strength and courage to love you and never leave the cross that you have chosen for me.

And bowing his head, he
handed over his spirit.
-from the Gospel of
St. John 19: 30

12
twelfth station

reflection by:
Brother Carlos Moreno, LC
artwork by:
M.D.
TIED Second-place Winner
3rd grade
Northwood Catholic School
Houston, TX, USA

reflection:

Loneliness. Christ dies alone. His disciples abandoned him and ran away. In the most important moment of our salvation Christ is alone. But he is alone because He wants to show his extreme love for me. He was not afraid to face death alone because He was thinking of me, and he wanted to teach me that love is stronger than death. How many times are we afraid to be alone? How many times before something that is very difficult for us do we feel alone? In these moments we should look up at the cross and see Christ Crucified. His love for me should give me the strength to overcome any difficulty, no matter how hard or frightening it may be. Christ from the cross is telling me: "Do not be afraid. I have died for you; because I love you in such a way that even death is nothing compared with your soul. I have suffered for you so that whenever you have to suffer, you may suffer in me and for me; and you will realize that in difficult times you are never alone; I am always with you."

my prayer to Jesus:

Thank you, Jesus, for showing me such love! Thank you for enduring loneliness in the difficult trial of your death on the cross! Help me to confront all the difficult moments of my life always at your side, so that I may not be afraid and be able to love you with all my heart as You have loved me.

Simeon blessed them and said to Mary his mother, "Behold, this child is destined for the fall and rise of many in Israel, and to be a sign that will be contradicted (and you yourself a sword will pierce) so that the thoughts of many hearts may be revealed."

-from the Gospel of St. Luke 2:34-35

JESUS IS TAKEN DOWN FROM THE CROSS

reflection by:
Brother Colin Gore, LC

artwork by:
Olivia
Third-place Winner
3rd grade
Blessed Sacrament School
Wichita, KS, USA

13

thirteenth station

reflection

His suffering is over now. After all the confusion of the last few hours, everything is quiet, and Christ hangs lifelessly from the cross, looking downward into empty space with eyes that used to be so full of love, but have now lost their twinkle. It seems impossible! The Son of God couldn't really be dead, or could he? ... Tears start rolling down my cheeks again since I don't want to believe that Jesus is truly gone. But as the nails are removed from his hands, his arms drop limply at his sides, and as we try to lower him gently downwards, he does not react when his body bumps the cross. I have no choice but to believe that his life with us is over. Right now I don't understand why this had to happen, but someday I will, and I will be overjoyed: Christ loved me so much that he died for me, so that I can be with him in heaven!

my prayer to Jesus:

Lord Jesus, although it is hard for me to believe that you truly died for me, help me to realize that your death was real, and that your resurrection was just as real. When people forget me and show me disrespect, help me remember that you loved me so much that you died for me, and for everyone else, too.

When it was evening, there came a rich man from Arimathea named Joseph... Taking the body, Joseph wrapped it in clean linen and laid it in his new tomb that he had hewn in the rock. Then he rolled a huge stone across the entrance to the tomb and departed. But Mary Magdalene and the other Mary remained sitting there, facing the tomb.

-from the Gospel of St. Matthew 27:57-61

reflection by:
Brother John Pietropaoli, LC

artwork by:
Shannon
Second-Place Winner
4th grade
Pinecrest Academy
Cumming, GA, USA

reflection:

When people die we feel terrible. We miss them, we wish we could see them again, and we know that something is wrong, that death is not right.

God the Father feels the same way, too. His only Son has just been killed in the most horrible way imaginable, and now his dead body is placed in a grave. The Father knows that something is wrong, that death is not right.

But He knows something else too: that death doesn't have the last word anymore. Jesus Christ rose from the dead, and gives us the promise of eternal life with him in heaven. Death is still real, and it's hard, but when Jesus died and rose from the dead he opened up the gates of heaven for us. And someday, when our life here is over, we will see Jesus and all those we've loved on earth; and nothing will ever be able

my prayer to Jesus:

Jesus, thank you for dying for me. Thank you for being such a loyal friend that you were willing to die for me, so that I could be with you forever in heaven. Thank you for never abandoning me—I know that you will never reject me, and that no matter how hard life is you will always be at my side. Please help me to be loyal to you, to live as you want me to live, and to help many other people come to know and love you too.

Special thanks to those who made this book possible:

Mrs. Keri Pye

Mrs. Lynn Dery

Ms. Mags Reilly

Mrs. Teri Marks

Mrs. Kerry Estes

Ms. Moira Gillott

Mrs. Karen Perry

Mr. Oscar Tanaka

Mrs. Kristin Jessen

Mrs. Kelly Luttinen

Mrs. Heather Kloer

Ms. Mary Degoede

Mrs. Carmelle Pilon

Ms. Anita Rittenburg

Mrs. Yamileth Rivera

Fr. Nathan Miller, LC

Mrs. Claudia Volkman

Mrs. Anne Holdsworth

Mrs. Romana Zia Khalaf

Br. Nicholas Sheehy, LC

Mrs. Stephanie DeRoche

Mrs. Seana Antee Tetzlaff

Br. Eduardo Quezada, LC

Mrs. Crystal Vanderbeek

Mrs. Mary Francis Skinner

Br Juan Pablo González, LC

Fourteen seminarians from the Legionaries of Christ

143 boys and girls who participated in the 2012 Stations of the Cross Drawing Contest

Thank You God.

Brother Peter Huynh, LC
Legionaries of Christ
Via degli Aldobrandeschi, 190
00163 Roma
ITALY
phuynh@legionaries.org

St. Thomas More Catholic School
630 West Ponce de Leon Avenue
Decatur, GA 30030
USA
www.stmga.org

Pinecrest Academy
955 Peachtree Parkway
Cumming, GA 30041
USA
www.pinecrestacademy.org

Northwoods Catholic School
5500 FM 2920
Spring, TX 77388
USA
www.northwoodscatholic.org

St. Thomas the Apostle
7303 Southwest 64th Street
Miami, FL 33143
USA
www.school.stamiami.org

St. John the Baptist Catholic School
350 Emery Street
Longmont, CO 80501
USA
www.v0.johnthebaptist.org

John Paul II Preparatory School
15977 Clayton Road
Ballwin, MO 63011
USA
www.johnpaulprep.org

Made in the USA
Lexington, KY
28 January 2017